TITYRUS

Praise for *Tityrus*

'I lost myself in this bittersweet sequence and it already feels like a place I've visited, a life I stowed-away in beyond the poems. A voice so compulsively readable, both tersely clear and compellingly mysterious that it gets into your head and starts narrating your own life.'
    — Luke Kennard

'Duncan Wiese's subversive pastoral *Tityrus* shows how fraught life has become for the Arcadian shepherds among us. Refusing to sugarcoat Tityrus's experience of our fetid and worn-out world, Wiese uncovers the daily pathos and absurdities of contemporary life. This spare yet encompassing verse narrative, deftly translated by Max Minden Ribeiro and Sam Riviere, provides an insightful and haunting portrait of our time.'
    — Denise Newman

'A pastoral where the shepherd not only grazes his sheep, but also himself, the human — where human and animal overlap in a current of medicine, food, myth, alcohol — and love. So right on time is Tityrus.'
    — Ursula Andkjær Olsen

'*Tityrus* reduces the distance between antiquity and the present moment in a single leap across the buck enclosure, and pastoral life becomes a matter of a delicate, organic-minded consciousness, a discussion of agricultural ethics and its capitalist principles, a hope for the future and a sensitive, youthful emotional life.'
— *ATLAS*

'*Tityrus* is something as unusual as pastoral poetry — a genre borrowed from the Roman poet Virgil. Not only is it paradoxical that Wiese, by so clearly following a historical literary tradition, has succeeded in creating a distinct voice entirely his own. With this double grip, he also shows that one does not arise out of nothing; one does not become something all by oneself.'
— Bogforum Prize for New Writing Jury

'Surprising, funny, utterly contemporary.'
— *Politiken*

Duncan Wiese

TITYRUS

A pastoral

Translated from Danish by
Max Minden Ribeiro & Sam Riviere

Lolli Editions
London

PROLOGUE

Where I come from
houses grow out of the ground
after rain
large stones grow
dark eggs
in the bedrock
kept

Mortar
Broken stone
Flour

The house is yellow with egg
my sisters are standing in the garden
red with blood
the dead hens
and dogs' teeth
in the grass
my mother
beams

Sons are slaughtered
before they grow up
in the house of the sun

VESTA

They lay in the green water and bobbed
the nanny sat by the shore and painted
she gathered flowers and laid them on the sand
then mixed the colours with water and made the paper wet
her hair was purple and short like the flowers on chives
the boys' pale bodies turned orange in the water
Tityrus paddled around looking down at his hands
like seeing the body of another beneath him
and the water thick and warm
they were so far out they avoided touching the bottom
soft and slimy and hidden there in the mud
were sharp stones twigs fishing hooks
lost things
and you only felt them
when you put your feet down to stand
and hoped
for the best

She couldn't hear them
but kept an eye out as she should
and shouted when they drifted out too far
they talked about the dead boy
who had drowned
close to the soldiers' bridge
Moelibus was the eldest of the two
and knew exactly where
his sister had shown him
he pointed to a place
where some small tired ducks
were looking up at the rushes

Later Moelibus said
the boy lived there

and pointed out towards the island

It was called Gull Island
there were often many gulls above it
like swarms of white bees
far away
and Tityrus thought
how it must be
to be dead and live on an island
with swarms of gulls
it was terrible
you could see the island
from the boy's old house
standing on the hill
over the lake
so they could look down on him
his father and mother
and he must be able to look back at them
when they turned the light on in the kitchen
and it was dark out on the island

One winter the lake froze
and there was so much snow
the men stayed in town
and drank beer
they couldn't come home
from work
it arrived suddenly
people abandoned their cars
and called on people they didn't know
and drank beer
the next day the cars
had vanished into new hills of snow
Tityrus crawled out the skylight
and jumped down to the yard
he dug a tunnel to the front door

and Vesta cheered from inside

They went down to the lake
with the dog and his sisters
they packed snacks and hot chocolate
Vesta wore skis
and shrieked as she skidded downhill

They ran across the lake
the dog in a wild sprint
the snow blew behind it like smoke
and Tityrus ran after
and he saw the thin grooves its claws
had scratched in the stiffened water
he stopped far out on the lake
the others still on their wild race
he gazed down into the green
he could see metres straight down
the sheet so thick
and he thought of the fish
wondered if they were dead
and Vesta came back to find him
and said the fish slept
when it was cold
and Tityrus thought of the raisins in squash cake
and wondered if the fish were alive
or if she was lying

They arrived at Gull Island
smaller than he'd thought
and there were no birds
only some shrubs
and low dry trees
and under the snow lay twigs
nests and stones
masses of plastic

yellow blue and white ribbons
knotted together
he thought of the boy
he did not believe that he lived here
here there was nothing
it was still
and deserted
on the island
the dog's tongue hung out steaming
big warm clouds over them
they drank hot chocolate and looked towards land
and Tityrus saw the house standing up on the hill
where the boy's family lived
they were quiet for a while
the dog lay down in the snow
and slept

Tityrus could see
the way they had come
in a green-black track
and he could see the hills
and he knew that behind them
stood the village
and in the village was his house
they were tired now
and walked slowly home

That night Tityrus dreamed
that he was sitting out on the island
with the warm dog
birds flying silent around him
like white leaves
he dreamed the air was full
of dandelion seeds and purple hair
across the water
the little boy came walking
Tityrus didn't dare wave
and when the boy reached the bank
he stretched out his orange hand
to Tityrus who woke
wet with sweat

the birds sang
day and night
by the light of the dead
and they lost feathers
from exhaustion
like sickly twigs
they dropped to the sand

pink beetles
shimmied
out of the ground

One day Tityrus sat on the back of a horse cart
and ate mini pizza rolls
and spat olive pits onto the lane
the parents had served up everything that could be drunk
collected from across the border in low trailers
that now stood sleeping in the carport
the only shady place
that summer
but no one emptied their drinks
they only took sips of the sweet liquid

The next day he sat on the back of a livestock trailer
it had been hosed down and hardly smelled
they went fast through the wind between the villages
and stopped outside gardens
sometimes he saw a lake he knew
and he grew ecstatic as they neared his pastures
he tried to explain to the Forester's Daughter
that it was here just here
he had run with the dog
that the lake by Soldiers' Bridge
was the lake where the little boy had drowned
and there in the forest
another boy's father had hung himself
from an oak tree
alone among the spruces

The house in the village had been sold
Vesta and Tityrus's father went their separate ways
the dog was dead and buried
she didn't listen but sang softly along
tilted her head and looked at Menacles
dancing with two redheaded girls

Tityrus understood and drank what he could
he filled his cheeks like two bags
the winds blew into the trailer and it rained a little
everyone got goosebumps and sang louder

The Forester's Daughter had on a Chanel dress
she sat on Tityrus's lap in the garden chair
and spoke about a man
who had rented a hotel room for her
down by the station
she told him about the food and the wine
the gifts
the things he did and knew
her muscular legs tensed
as she spoke and Tityrus remembered
spraining a muscle the day he tried
to race her one winter
he had heard the stories before
about the other boys and men
and loved what she said
the secret
places and light
things presents food
the bodies
how they looked naked
he had lain below her
in his father's bed
she said
this is how

and began to move
I like it
and that was all it was
then they slept

In the evening up in the attic
she kissed Menacles's sharp mouth
he kissed her back
until she was bursting
then he pushed her away
and went down the stairs
and back to the city

Tityrus saw it all
he sat and watched
the girl from the forest
was angry
she wanted to smash
the young men's faces
everything young she hated
everything the young men couldn't do

She unpacks him
and says
you can stay here

The big blood beech
in the middle of the courtyard
rises above the rooves
like a skyscraper
a grand hotel
of densely woven branches
once in a while
a kitten falls
to the gravel
a dull thud
like ripe fruit

They wake in the night
and talk
come crusted around them
like sleep
she gets up first
and brushes her hair
in the dark
at the mirror
as the light rouses
old and slow
in the bulb
like the ghost of her forebears
on the farm
her brushing sounds like dry bread
he rises slowly
and puts his warmth
into T-shirt and jeans

The darkness between the trees
on the lane
is filled
with sounds
mice tumble around
and wrestle each other
delighting in the frost
white and warm
it shines
between the furrows
a sea
crusted
beneath their feet
they both warm themselves
on Tityrus's body
while the sky
little by little
thaws
first white
then yellow
then red

The tip of the sunbeam hits the white sock
on the windowsill
folded in an arc
facing the light
and last night he had wiped the come
off his belly
and thrown it there
and now it's shining
like a little bowl of light

Tityrus runs slowly like an old man
on gooseberry legs and with a tight painful ball
for a belly
he sprints into the row of hazels
grown together over the path
a hollow bush
once in a while the sun hits Tityrus
and he springs
past his shadow

The path is the backstage of the great agricultural theatre
the sun that persistently sings for its children
they grow and turn yellow
in the long hot summer
until harvest
when men like death
drive humming over the field

The mute agricultural machines on the horizon
have small bonfires inside them
like all animals people and cars
they wait in great barns
in the shadows they stand dripping and creaking

The pain disappears from his stomach
and on the hill he picks up pace
he has taken a fitness test
he is at level zero
but he still has soldier dreams

He dreamed that he lived in a big house
of red brick
that had only one room
like a church
he lived with his comrades
the war was over
but anyway the house caved in on them
in their sleep
a bombing raid
it was the young women
thought Tityrus
they had come after the fire
and said
they couldn't be lovers
any longer
not with the danger
he posed
was it the girls
he thought
was it them
that did it

Tityrus walks out on the field
he tenses all of his muscles
he shakes and sweat squirts
from his forehead
his thoughts let slide
the important formulas
and then he lights up the sky
with his little sword

Tityrus walks under the treetops
he slips in the mud and grabs a branch
the forest is soon replaced by a campsite
a young girl with a dog smiles at
him between the hedges she is on holiday
Tityrus hurries along the road past the kiosk
a sullen hum hangs over the asphalt
like invisible insects
Tityrus finds the path to the forest again
and sees a large transformer substation
its towers like grey mushrooms
it's them making the noise
and he thinks
this is a machine
that converts
something into something
like trees are machines
that convert energy from the sun
and nutrients from the earth
an engine that burns
and grows upward

Tityrus is a comparison machine
he sees two snails feeding on
a third snail
not quite dead yet
and Tityrus thinks it looks a lot like
the small windows on porn sites
with bronze coloured bodies sliding
in and out of each other
Tityrus speeds up
Menacles writes that he is
on his way

Tityrus starts to run
sprints past some tourists
and he finds
a long rotten beech stick
and breaks it off at a suitable length

Tityrus walks with the walking stick
like a shepherd in the woods
he sits down at the forest's edge
facing the beach
huge trees line the shore
a seagull struggles
with a crab and flaps up frightened
and Tityrus is ashamed
to have disturbed its meal
the gull glides fast
low over the water
wrah wrah wrah
Tityrus knows how awful it is
to be disturbed while eating
it is like having a body part carved
from the future's body
that's what food is
something you're about to become

Tityrus works with a penknife into the stick
he peels the grey bark
beneath the flesh is blackened with rot
Tityrus carves a handle
completely white
this is approx. the width of my hand he thinks
and he is right

Tityrus manages to carve
a T an I a T and a Y
before Menacles calls

he's standing outside the forest
Tityrus runs again
under the treetops
he stops at the iron age graveyard
and lies among the approx. 28 burial mounds
Tityrus sees emeralds glinting in the moss
and an ancient family of mosquitoes pierces his skin

Menacles calls now and coaxes
Tityrus into saying where he is lying
the baby blue Citroën brakes hard
on the gravel track

Menacles gets out and the door slams
like a shot between the trunks
he walks over
tall and fair with stubble glinting
on his face and he sits down
beside Tityrus
he offers him a cigarette
and asks
what's going on here?

Tityrus answers
nothing much

Moelibus is sitting on the stairs
with a large glass of coffee
up on the hill stands the King's Stable
like a red ox
made cold and dark by the night
the sky is turquoise and thin
yellow at the edges and a strip of exhaust
crosses from one bank to the other

His skin is warm and red
the bottles on the table
standing and lying
like a little town
the bottletops and cig butts
girls and boys on their way home

His crooked nose
and his black hair
marvellously tousled
the whites of his eyes
drawn through with red threads
the night has sewn him a face
and the girl from the art academy is lying
naked on the bed
next to the boxes of cameras

Tityrus comes in from the kitchen
his bag heavy with books
then he stops
by the stairs
and says good morning

Moelibus sobs

Why are you crying?
asks Tityrus

He doesn't know
he's tired

Tityrus sits down on the stairs
and cries a little

He saw the porpoises
as black arcs
they rose up
and down
halves

They moved
silently along the coast
and were gone
the wind still blew
and it rained
but the boys were motionless
they had stood for a long time
watching them

They stood
on the wet rocks
and really they had meant to
pick sea kale
and mussels
and fish

But the porpoises
appeared

And then Tityrus said
did you see the porpoises?

They cross the road
to the sons
on the neighbour's land
they were sexually mature
after three months
now a year has passed
and they've grown beards
and short fat horns
on their foreheads
we slaughter the sons
and keep the daughters
that's farming
they stink and their fleece
sticks to the fingers
incessantly the largest
attempts to mate
with the smallest
what a program
pure drive for twelve months
then a shiny metal ball
through the forehead

They go round to the neighbour's garden
under the old walnut tree
they begin to collect
the beautiful little coffins
that the tree's children lie in
so the wind
to slip
and fall
all is hope
of reproduction
to sling your seed

32

drop eggs to the earth
and long for the new
a healthy child
if there is such a thing
flesh cut from yourself
flesh that wanders

Slowly in the twilight
they fill the white bucket
as in childhood at the edge of the wood
blackberries
night's rubies

He washes the tree's children
in a plastic tub at the table
the water turning black
he drains it three times
now it's red
they sing
when he pours the hot water over them
a weak sound
as it seeps into the coffin
their bodies drenched
maybe the heat was a mistake
maybe they're ruined

He tears one open
and eats the grey brains
the nuts stabilise his mood
like the pills

Tityrus bakes lavender biscuits
in his mother's kitchen
he goes onto the heath
and buys two bright blue jars from the ceramicist
he is thinking about

the queen of dreams and the Doctor in the city
he sees his Oma and the woman from the heath
wandering through the darkness
his closed eyes spark
while he drinks his coffee
in the yellow light under the lamp
he pays for the jars with cash
and fills them with nuts
and takes them with him
he sits on the train
with his gifts
in the hope of a final reconciliation
a life with many daughters
and few sons

THE DOCTOR

The apartment smells of soap shavings
a new life
the withered tomato plant stands on the windowsill
a black little tree
with two red fruit

Tityrus unwraps the jars
and sets them on the table
another gift for the Doctor
she hasn't asked for
Titryus feels ashamed
she's sleeping in the other room
he's sitting quietly on the sofa

The garbage bag lies on the floor
a pale film around colourful cartons
the gut of the apartment
it digests what they cannot

She left it for him this morning
when she went to work
there it is
waiting
as is the shepherd
under the covers

Beside the white shoes
some brown fluid runs out

The dirty dishes stand in the light from the yard
that hangs in the kitchen
that hangs in the bedroom

Tityrus saw a magpie on the ledge
when he finally got up
he would say
they made eye contact
but it flew off

Tityrus washes up
out in the hallway hangs an oval mirror
the mirror shows Tityrus who washes up
his body bare to the waist
the grey and white stripes of his swimming trunks
in the violet light from the courtyard

A sickness in Tityrus
makes him quiet and distant
smiling and unapproachable
like the orchids
in the windows
he sits on the stool
hot and tired

The Doctor is sleeping under a double duvet
Tityrus lies down on the sheepskin rug in the living room

Tityrus is looking for jobs online
there are no positions for shepherds
Tityrus applies for a job as a receptionist

He will tend to memos
like goats
and breed meetings
pick ballpoint pens as he murmurs
a calming song

Why does your heart beat like that Tityrus?

Down on the street
people move
some pick up bread
like ants

There goes the Doctor
in the sun
she has khaki shorts
and a white shirt
and that is her bicycle

Tityrus is a clammy heart lying on the sofa
blood that's pumped round the apartment

He's trying to send signals
out into the world
scents and text messages
he writes hi
nothing else

The beautiful guard on the psychiatric emergency ward
is wearing all black
car keys hanging from his belt
he is the right age the right build
muscles under the fabric of his T-shirt
the sunbed has buffed his face
to a lustrous bronze
and also the way
he walks in and the way he leaves again
reverses into the parking bay
and accelerates out
like that
quickly
in a V
V for Victor
in and out of the day
like no other

The plywood furniture is geology
an exhibition of the tree's interior
grain like script
long slender letters

The Ritalin works
the salami and the tomato
the cross-section of them shows
two logical constructions
logic is gorgeous
society wants for nothing
the tomato has two chambers
like the heart
they are filled with jelly and seeds
society just exists
are there seeds in Tityrus's heart
do they grow
is it difficult to breathe
and think
he eats air
in summer his lungs are pollinated
he draws breath in
and everything else with it
the tomato and the salami have a skin
the stone has a shell
slice through and it is a vessel
crowded with crystals

The blue morning
breaks the light
of the cars' eyes
the inevitable days
cross the street

46

The Doctor wants to leave Tityrus
Tityrus wants to leave the Doctor
The Doctor doesn't want to leave Tityrus
Tityrus doesn't want to leave the Doctor

Along the way the Doctor cries
so does Tityrus

Tityrus gets up from the table
he goes out and puts the kettle on
if she comes back
there is tea
if not
there is still tea

Everyone mistreats each other
no one gives in
it's summer
the flying ants hatch
and colonise dreams

Tityrus smokes a joint with Ø and Fabrikken
they walk through Frederiksberg
and duck under clusters of lilacs
which smell pink like boys' bodies
Ø plays dance music on his iPhone

Down by the canal
on the large stones
they light up another
and time transforms into plates
that Tityrus lands on
between vast spaces
of nothing

They meet Trommen in the yard
he asks Ø if they should perform
and they go up on stage
and everyone gasps
and screams with delight
Fabrikken buys soda
for him and Tityrus
Tityrus knows
it's happening now
the insane pull
down
down towards sorrow
earth
and the sweat lifts
like flies from his forehead
his mouth bleats
soon combines
what's within
with what's without

50

He gets up from the chair
shaking as he walks
and treads and treads
on what
his feet can find
and unlocks the door
to the toilet

Far inside the house without windows
there lies a shepherd
on the floor

The mirror has given way
and Tityrus throws up

Long
this is how it always feels
long as never before
always long
it goes on
seeping from the shepherd's mouth

In the basin they lie
white as asparagus
the children who were just inside him
and they are not his
to cherish any longer

Tityrus sobs
and cries out from the floor
but the house is quiet
sirens from the street
creep under the door
small red oxen
nudge his forehead
confused animals

And Tityrus thinks
now is a good time to die
he slips down between the tiles
and lies under the floor
like when the hay bales
collapsed over the two boys
in the barn
and he thought then
now is a good time to die
the same
thing he thought at the festival
on the grass
when he disappeared
and no one saw that he drowned
in the ground
before the Doctor came running
and cried
on his black cheeks and drenched clothes
there was earth between his teeth
he was outside himself
on his way into the world
and they pumped life
in through the skin
again

and he thought so
alone
in the hospital
years later
with the tubes
and the faces of the nurses
like the loveliest of icons
only offering light
salt and water
and thick whole milk
in white plastic cups

that now
was a good time to die
he was so happy
to lie
there

On the floor of the house
the beetles giggle
they're so happy
in their pink bodies
paper falls from the wall
like water from heaven
and Tityrus sticks his hands
under the warm whiteness
now again he is their
little shepherd boy

Ø sits alone on a chair
and listens to the room
Tityrus says hi
and Ø says welcome back
and Tityrus says to Ø
I'm going home
and Ø says
that he'll come too

They walk under the streetlamps
in the city's great front room
Ø's face lights up
as he speaks about poisonous plants
and Tityrus says
that he has never really
loved death
only girls
and Ø says nothing
as the ambulance bursts past

in a light blue shriek
and Ø smiles
and nods
as if all is well again

A NEW SUN

The shirts on hangers in the window
apparitions of days that have past
warnings of what is to come

Tityrus stands in the forest
his pocket hums
it's the Poet
the lilac mouth blooms everywhere on the phone
and on the forest floor
ears filled with spit
and the tongue
inside him

His fingers dig out small stones
until the blood seeps out
between the rocks
he paints red circles
on her breasts

What did it mean Tityrus
which sun
what should you give up
the many days alone with goats weren't spent alone
they were filled with true sentences
and you pointed at what you desired
and it fell from heaven
and who he thought
with branches in bundles
dares to go to town without jewellery and promises
newly purchased liquids
who dares to even speak to a human being
apart from those
who are not afraid to die
or lose everything
and what do you even have to offer
quiet and still shepherd boy in the woods
a lilac shirt

heavy lips
and a body steeped in the whitest medicine

Tityrus lay down on the forest floor and pulled off his trousers
so he could disappear
down through the centuries' leaves
short filthy poems and beloved stones
text messages like horny birds
that burst
each morning
on the sky
the sheets brown and white
streaks of blood

Now the sun tore loose and everything rained
He licked his hand
and thought of the Poet

He pulled up his trousers and tied the white cord
he collected the last logs
and put them on the pile

The forest is just like the city
I didn't believe you
but I pick scarletina mushrooms
and ceps in parks and churchyards now

Tityrus stands with Menacles
in someone's living room
he dances with the long body
like seagrass over the little stones
in the sand and mussels
they ash and talk over each other
with bottles in their pockets
like cyclists and they
are such good friends
thinks Tityrus
and he thinks
Menacles is the only one
I want to dance with
and the girls slink in between them
and tweak Menacles's belly under his thin shirt
and he is so sad Tityrus wants to cry
and hurt the girl who hurt his friend
and then
Menacles lowers his eyes
towards the feet and empty cans
and says
I have to go home
and Tityrus nods and says ok
I'll stay
and Menacles finds his bike outside
while Tityrus dances
and distributes his medication to strangers
who become lethargic and greedy
while Tityrus becomes more and more restless
and finds his jacket
under the jackets
the sleeve in a bucket
wet as a cheek

and on the way down the stairs
Tityrus thinks
he only wants to dance with Menacles
and he calls the Poet
his pockets are empty
his medication has run out
and he goes home gently
to her

Every morning Tityrus fills his stomach again

dry white bread
2 cups of coffee
a glass of water and cheese and butter
20 mg Ritalin
his eyes are big and black when he wakes
they go small and white when
the medicine dissolves inside him
one thing at a time
he lies cramping in the garden
it comes to him
one thing at a time
while all the garden's siblings shout at him

He is empty when he comes back to himself
and reads sporadically in the encyclopaedia
Ion, The Ionian Islands
Ionisation: the charge of air molecules
Iran
Iraq
he's leafing
the caravan smells heavy with sleep

The Poet draws a section of garden outside the window
and suddenly he sees himself in grey and black lines:

Tityrus reading the encyclopaedia
naked under the duvet like a sculpture of a shepherd
the wakeful Tityrus
the arm strong and beautiful
face small and dark
they get up and come seeps out of her

they laugh a little and both feel sick
it wells and swells in the little room
and they tumble out into the sun

Tityrus thinks:
unable to deal with having emptied himself
into another and having to see and smell and hear himself
in another's body
there is no coherance under the medicine's regime
only the separate and singular
clear distinct forms
like the Poet's drawings
she slowly sets
the singulars together
as a thing
him
a person
or a landscape
some areas magnified
distended
her eyes rest on something a while and it grows
the gable
the flower
the arm

Tityrus's glances collect
around small signs
the scar on the stomach
like a T
the small yellow tuft
above her sex
her transparent eyebrows
reading
Io
white heifer that founded a people

Tityrus looks at the lavender
but his head swims at all the purple cups
and bumblebees that tumble drunk
from cask to cask

Grief is losing
or not getting what you want
the cry is the hungry mouth
shame is the quiet wind
in the sand
anxiety is the forest
anger is the plain
under the beat of running feet

Joy is the pale bun
they share out in front of the kiosk
and semen on the neck's construction
and what she says
and what you refuse to give
all the rules that constitute life
Titryus sticks his fingers in under the blonde tuft
the light dry skull groans
the fingers find their way through the flesh
everything that has happened is the body
now now it frays
now the last threads
bloody and meaningless
everything that constitutes a life
the sun behind cloud cover
sees the world
a grey loaf
big and solid
as agriculture
there'll be nothing more
it's all the same
and she says
with fingers in her mouth
it doesn't matter

They watch *The Walking Dead*
someone eats someone else
someone loses their life
and returns
as the truth
a slow and shambling gait
a clutching hunger
the snails drawn over the asphalt
do they have purpose
will the cities open their gates
will they lift your arms
and offer you their sons
do they know
that you are a good man
the best there is
a line of rubbed chalk
do they know
that your rooms are true
like longing
sorry dear one
sorry beloved
sorry to you
shepherd friend

Do you think
that I'll survive
do we think
that there is
a word
a quiet waste
where no one lives
do you think
friend
that the will of the trees
the quiet trickle
outside the window

is a language
do you think
there is a place
the plain
the forest
where the true is true
and not beautiful
where coins
and cigarettes
rain from the sky
you just click
and naked children
are denied nothing
where no commerce
is worth more than the sand
that crunches between teeth
where the sun's sisters dance like
you my elastic brother
and where what we see
is what there is
nothing else!
the future is dew
and fog over the field
you!
see the blood red sky
it calls
to you
and me
the last
of the plain's
children
it's now
come come
dear friend
there is no more
to eat

no more
to do
no more meat
no more now

Come

Out

The

Sun

Bleeds

As

A

New

Sun

Now

EPILOGUE

Early mornings on buses
pheasants waking at dawn

My dad doesn't exist in dreams
he walks in the forest
with his chainsaw

The big parties
lights in the streets
every night
a birthday
some dreams
are close as death
the wakeful
tired as the day
sleep is a salve
work is a sore
that stays open

In cars
on trains
on buses
I'm carried by the dreams of others
into the language of others
on the carriage floor
a playing card
a 10
a tiger
at night
strokes my foot
cat's eyes
in the dark kitchen
two bright green holes
see me

When we slaughtered chickens
it stank of iron fruits
the dry pipe
that snapped in the rooster's throat
yellow eyes ruined in the grass
the tree stump sticky
and black
all winter
fine down stuck fast
deep in the grain

Will new chickens bloom
in the black tree
like the Judas ear
purple and translucent
young blood vessels
on the dead skin

I shot the pheasant through its yellow eye
and the field mouse writhed
on the hard ground
until the blood
boiled by lead
settled
in tiny black drops

The electric hum
from the slaughterhouse in the valley
woke me again tonight

They tore it down last year
and built a house on top

The whole time on the train
and in town
I tire myself thinking
exhaustion and discipline
are my truest wish

It's easy
to hurt others
I dream of dying
with some
conscience

The whole time the sun
has really been there
as a friend to me
today

I swim back and forth in the pool

I ride the train back and forth between cities

In the gaps between arrivals
I swim
I sit

My father is tired
the medicine is working

That's the idea
the immune system
attacks the cancer
the cancer is a part of him
that has run riot
the medicine is trying to trick him
into believing
the cancer is foreign
the risk is that
he believes everthing is foreign
and the white blood cells
tear him down

He looks sad
his arms are getting thinner
my strong father

It feels like a kind of suicide
but I don't say that
at first I thought it was a good idea
but now I see
that he is dying in front of me
and I can't do anything
and writing about it
removes him from me

I was a religious child
I prayed as I cycled
for all sorts of things
money
sweets
a magical Gameboy
with all the world's games on it
I prayed not to die completely
but to be reborn as a sorceror
or a Pokémon trainer
I prayed not to be found
in school
I prayed for the safety of my sisters
I prayed for my mother to be happy

Did I pray for my dad?
When I was smallest
he was big as a god
his hands enormous
they could crush a skull
heft a city
now he is disappearing
and I love him
more and more

I listen to loud music
for several hours
every morning
drowning out my prayers
I wasn't christened
I don't know who I think
I'm talking to

He drinks beer with us boys
and we have sausages and cider
it's not many years ago

down at the dairy
in the forest
that we worked together
for some years we were almost equally strong
then I went back to school
and my body became light
and his became heavier and heavier
until now

I'm sitting in a classroom
at university writing
no one's showed up
I mean
apart from me
the car park outside is hard to describe
so many cars
trees and sometimes
people
that move
on different routes
like invisible tunnels
drawing purpose
nothing escapes the earth
I carry myself around
like a bag of soil
and there are the green buses to the station
today I arrived in this room
this chair
this is far from empty
I'm just the only person
sitting here right now

An oak tree stands outside the window
they must not be felled
that's the rule
the other trees
the white birch
especially
those are felled
there is a hierarchy
Oak
Beech
Ash
Hawthorn
Pine

probably others
before we arrive at birch
it is invasive
growing fast
spreading surface roots
so they topple in storms
as if a giant hand
has pressed them down

The window opens
with a low sucking sound
and closes again
then I think
he is dead

But he isn't
as far as I know

I don't want to know
I go down for a swim

The swimming pool is closed
I buy cigarettes in the canteen
and borrow a lighter

Two girls come out of the university
and one says:
priests are human too
and they laugh and smoke

DUNCAN WIESE (b. 1991) is a Danish poet and a graduate of the Danish Academy of Creative Writing, where he now teaches. He is the author of two poetry books, and his debut, *Tityrus*, was shortlisted for the prestigious Bodil and Jørgen Munch-Christensen Prize and the Bogforum Prize for New Writing. He lives in Funen.

MAX MINDEN RIBEIRO is a literary translator and academic philosopher. His recent publications include Pelle Hvenegaard's *Dear Zoe Ukhona* and *Finn Juhl: Life, Work, World* by Christian Bundegaard. He lives in Copenhagen.

SAM RIVIERE is the author of three poetry books: *81 Austerities, Kim Kardashian's Marriage,* and *After Fame,* and most recently a novel, *Dead Souls* (2021).

This translation was made possible through the generous support of the Danish Arts Foundation, the Fondation Jan Michalski, and Konsul George Jorck & Hustru Emma Jorck's Fond

A CIP catalogue record for this book is available from the British Library

ISBN 978-1-915267-15-3

Lolli Editions
New Wing, 44
Somerset House
Strand
London WC2R 1LA
United Kingdom
www.lollieditions.com